Positive Mindset
JOURNAL

Written by Jennifer Bashant, Ph.D.

Designed by Overit

This Journal Belongs To:

_____

Contents

Your Happy Place 2

Hopes & Dreams 8

Relaxation 14

Gratitude 20

Giving Back 26

What Brings You Joy? 32

Inspiration 38

Connection To Others 44

Healthy Habits 50

Celebrate Your Success 56

Your Happy Place

No matter what is happening around you, there is always a place of calm and peacefulness you can go to in your mind. Being able to find this place when you are stressed can be challenging but it gets easier with practice. Your happy place may be somewhere you have already been or a place you dream of visiting. When you visit your happy place, you can feel the same happy vibes as if you were actually there!

Give it a try!

Close your eyes...

take a deep breath and feel every cell in your body relax, from the top of your head, all the way down to your toes... and then

...imagine your happy place.

(Let's call this zen dreaming)

What do you see?

Check in with your other senses... Describe any sounds, scents, or tastes in your happy place:

How do you feel?

What other places make you feel this way?

_____
_____
_____
_____
_____
_____
_____
_____

Will you do this zen dreaming again? Why?

_____
_____
_____
_____
_____
_____
_____
_____

Imagining all the descriptive words you've just written, DRAW

Your Happy Place

right here in this space!

Hopes & Dreams are expressions of our potential and help you discover and develop your talents. They help to steer and shape your life choices.

What are some of your Hopes & Dreams?

List your hopes here:

Dream Big!
List your dreams here:

What are some of your special talents, and how can you use them to make your dreams become a reality?

What actions can you take to move you closer to your hopes and dreams?

How will your life change when your dreams come true? How will you feel?

Color this dream catcher in your favorite colors while imagining all of your hopes and dreams coming true. Live as if they are already here, and they will reach you faster!

Relaxation

Stress is a normal part of life, and something everyone experiences. But stress can get out of control, leaving you feeling sad, angry, or overwhelmed. Learning how to relax, then building that into your day will help you keep your stress level low. With a little practice, managing your stress will become easier as you learn to listen to your body and heed its warning signals.

One way to relax is to use a breathing technique that works for you. Here's one you can try:

4 - 7 - 8 Breathing Technique

Before starting, get comfortable, either sitting or lying down.

Focus on the following breathing pattern:

- Empty your lungs of air
- Breathe in quietly through your nose for 4 seconds
- Hold your breath for 7 seconds
- Exhale through your nose for 8 seconds
- Repeat as many times as needed until your body and mind begin to calm

Now, how do you feel?

_____
_____
_____
_____
_____
_____
_____
_____
_____
_____
_____
_____

How can you tell that you are stressed?

_____
_____
_____
_____
_____
_____
_____
_____
_____

Where do you notice stress in your body?

_____
_____
_____
_____
_____
_____
_____
_____
_____

What are your favorite ways to relax?

Recall a time you were stressed and what you did to relax yourself:

Circle your favorite ways to relax.

Talk with Friends	Garden	Day Dream
Do Yoga	Take a Walk	Go for a Run
Listen to Music	Read	Meditate
Take a Nap	Draw	Sit in Nature
Count the Stars	Journal	Pet Your Dog

Doodle Space!

Grat·i·tude

> Gratitude, thankfulness, or gratefulness, from the Latin word gratus 'pleasing, thankful,' is a feeling of appreciation felt or shown by the recipient of kindness, gifts, help, favors, or other types of generosity, towards the giver of such gifts.

Practicing gratitude has been shown to improve mood, self-esteem, physical health, and create stronger friendships.

Gratitude brings a sense of peace to your soul that only comes when you truly are thankful; when you are ready to show appreciation and return kindness.

What are you grateful for?

Who are you grateful for and why?

List five positives you notice today:

1.

2.

3.

4.

5.

When you practice gratitude each day, how does that improve your life?

Describe a time when you used gratitude to change how you felt:

Draw what gratitude looks like to you here.

Giving Back

Did you know that helping others actually makes you feel happier? When you give back, you become more aware of those in need, as well as your infinite ability to help.

10 benefits of...

Giving Back

1. It is good for your health
2. It gives you a sense of purpose
3. It helps you meet new people
4. It deepens your sense of community
5. It unlocks your hidden skills
6. It shares your expertise with others
7. It helps you gain a new perspective
8. It helps you grow
9. It improves your mood
10. It boosts your self-esteem

Which of the above benefits do you want to feel more often and how will you achieve that?

_____
_____
_____
_____
_____
_____
_____
_____
_____
_____
_____

What are some of the ways you have given your time or resources?

In what other ways would you like to give back?

Describe the feeling you get when you give back.

Using colored pencils, crayons, markers, or paint, show the colors that your heart feels when you give back.

What brings you
JOY?

Finding Joy

When life is hectic and you have a lot to do, it is easy to be so focused on completing tasks that you forget to slow down and enjoy the small pleasures of each day. Every time you feel happy and take a minute to soak in those good vibes, you are rewiring your brain to be happier. Your brain is always growing and changing based on how you use it and where you decide to focus your attention.

What are some of the things that bring you joy each day?

_____
_____
_____
_____
_____
_____
_____
_____

What people, pets, activities or places bring you the most joy?

What do you want to pay more attention to because it will make you feel happy?

How would you describe the difference between joy and happiness?

Spend some time drawing or doodling while you reflect on what brings you joy.

Inspiration

Inspiration is a feeling of enthusiasm you get from someone or something, that sparks creative ideas. That enthusiasm and sense of purpose is what will get you motivated to take action toward reaching your goals.

What activities or hobbies do you take part in that inspire you?

Name one person you find inspiring and describe why.

Is there a place in your home or somewhere else where you feel inspired to be creative?

Recall a time when you felt inspired. What triggered it and how did you feel?

Take a photograph of something or someone inspiring, then print the photo and attach it here.

Connection to Others

Humans are social beings, wired for connection. Having deep, meaningful connections to others is a major factor in your happiness. Positive social relationships protect you from the negative effects of stress and make you feel happier.

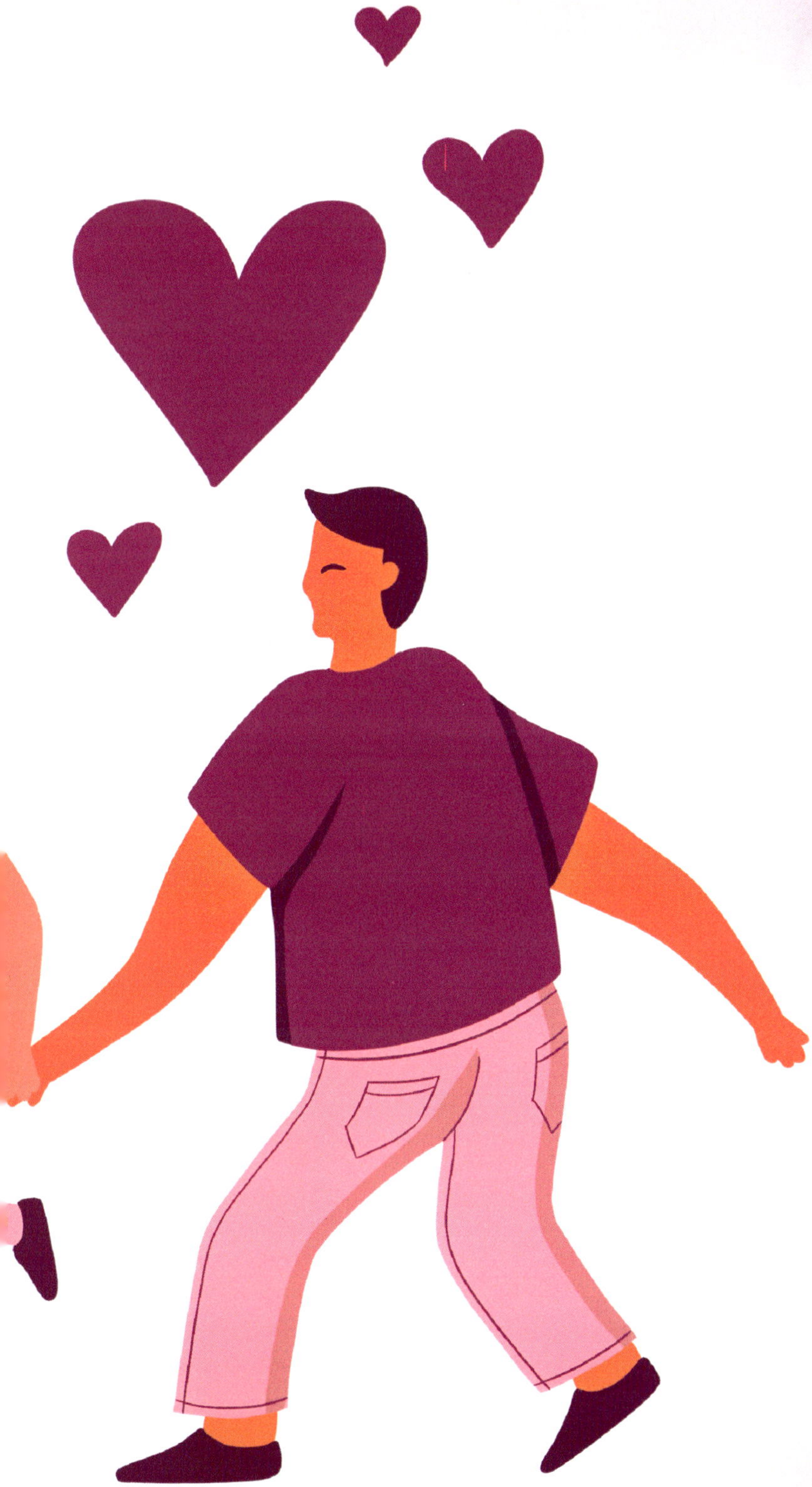

Describe some of your closest friends and what you love about each person.

Sometimes life takes us on different paths and and we lose touch with friends from certain times in our lives.

Is there someone you miss and have lost touch with, and how will you reconnect?

What are some of your favorite things to do with friends?

Doodle Space!

"We first make our habits, then our habits make us"

– John Dryden

Healthy Habits

There are many types of habits that can lead to a healthier mind and body, but let's start by considering your habits around nutrition, exercise, sleep and setting boundaries. On the next pages, list the healthy habits you already have in each area, then describe any additional habits you would like to develop.

Habits I Already Have:

Nutrition

Type of food, amount, quality, timing

Exercise

Type, frequency, duration

Sleep
Quality, duration

Setting Boundaries
Saying no, work/home boundaries, advocating for self, using your voice

Habits I Would Like to Form:

Nutrition
Type of food, amount, quality, timing

Exercise
Type, frequency, duration

Sleep
Quality, duration

Setting Boundaries
Saying no, work/home boundaries, advocating for self, using your voice

Celebrate Your Success!

Research shows that when you take the time to appreciate how far you have come and celebrate your successes, you are actually rewiring your brain to be more positive. Look for ways in which you are growing and improving each day, then acknowledge and celebrate the achievement of your goals. Seeing your own progress is motivating and will encourage you to keep going. Each time you set a goal, be sure to build in how you will measure your progress, and how you will know when you have accomplished your goal.

What was one success you had this week?

How did you acknowledge or celebrate this success?

Describe a goal you have for yourself, and how you will know when you have achieved it.

Draw what success looks like to you in this space.

시원해!